OFFICIALLY
WITHDRAWN

The editors would like to thank
BARBARA KIEFER, Ph.D.,
Charlotte S. Huck Professor of Children's Literature,
The Ohio State University, and
TRICIA EDWARDS,
Head of Education, Lemelson Center for the Study of Invention and Innovation,
National Museum of American History, Smithsonian Institution,
for their assistance in the preparation of this book.

Visit us on the Web!
Seussville.com
randomhousekids.com

Educators and librarians, for a variety of teaching tools, visit us at
RHTeachersLibrarians.com

Library of Congress Cataloging-in-Publication Data
Worth, Bonnie, author.
Oh, the things they invented! : all about great inventors / by Bonnie Worth ; illustrated by
Aristides Ruiz and Joe Mathieu. — First edition.
    pages   cm. — (The Cat in the Hat's learning library)
Summary: "From the wheel to the World Wide Web—the Cat in the Hat looks at inventors and
inventions that have changed our lives." —Provided by publisher.
Audience: Ages 5–8.
ISBN 978-0-449-81497-0 (trade) — ISBN 978-0-375-97170-9 (lib. bdg.)
1. Inventions—History—Juvenile literature. 2. Inventors—History—Juvenile literature. I. Ruiz,
Aristides, illustrator. II. Mathieu, Joe, 1949– illustrator. III. Title. IV. Series: Cat in the Hat's
learning library.
T15.W83 2015 609—dc23 2014029190

Printed in the United States of America
10 9 8 7 6 5

OH, THE THINGS THEY INVENTED!

by Bonnie Worth

illustrated by Aristides Ruiz and Joe Mathieu

The Cat in the Hat's Learning Library®

Random House 🏠 New York

I'm the Cat in the Hat,
and as everyone knows,
I'm a cat who is fond
of machines and gizmos.

All through human history
(since before the year one),
things have been invented
to help get stuff done.

Tools improve daily life,
and I think you will find
they are fabulous products
of the human mind!

SUPER-DEE-D
INVENTION CON

The inventors of tools,
from old and new ages,
will now spring to life
in these very pages.

If you're ready to meet them,
please turn your attention
to the Super-dee-Duper
Invention Convention!

JOHANNES GUTENBERG
around 1439
MOVABLE-TYPE PRINTING PRESS

Gutenberg (GOO-ten-berg),
who worked with metals like gold,
found a way to print books
that improved on the old.

Before, books were copied
by hand—this is so.
The pace of these scribes
was incredibly slow.

Or pages were carved out
of one wooden block,
then inked and pressed down
onto smooth paper stock.

A book took forever
to make, and that's why
books were for rich folks
alone to go buy.

Gutenberg's metal letters,
both capital and small,
periods and commas
and colons and all,
were laid out word by word,
by the page in a tray,
locked in, and then copied
in ink in this way.

Page after page,
he laid each out anew,
printing 200 Bibles
before he was through!

His printing machine—
you never will guess—
was made from a very old
unused winepress!

JAMES WATT—1769
MODERN
STEAM
ENGINE

Perhaps young James Watt
watched a teakettle steam,
and there got the spark for
his steam engine dream.

Did he see the effect
that boiled water brings?
The steam creates power
that then can move things.

To make matters clear,
the Things will now show
how a steam engine works.
Turn the page and you'll know.

Water heats in a boiler
until it makes steam.
Then steam
leaves the boiler
in a powerful stream.

It enters a cylinder,
causing pistons to go.

PISTON

But when the steam cools,
the pistons will slow.

Before Watt, steam engines
did not work well at all.
When the hot steam cooled down,
the pistons would stall.

Watt took the cooled steam
(turned to water by then)
and pumped it back to the boiler
to heat up again.

Factory machines
kept chugging this way,
and steam locomotives
could choo-choo all day.

ELI WHITNEY
1793 COTTON GIN

To separate fibers
from the cotton plant's seeds
took many hands picking,
for long hours indeed!

Mr. Whitney's all-new
cotton-sorting machine
turned a slow, dirty job
into one quick and clean.

COTTON LINT

SEED

CLEAN COTTON

METAL SCREEN holds back SEEDS

COTTON with SEEDS

SEEDS

The gin used a screen,
and it worked simply to
hold the seeds back while hooks
pulled the cotton lint through.

A big moving brush
cleared the lint to make way
for the next round of cotton.
Why, that gin ran all day!

LOUIS DAGUERRE

The convention's next star,
standing right next to me?
Daguerre, who helped make
the first photography!

He based it on a clever
and ancient gizmo
called the camera obscura,
which we will now show.

Daguerre
(duh-GARE)

It's a box with a hole,

and it makes Thing One frown,

tiny hole to let in light

LIGHT

LIGHT

LIGHT

LIGHT

LIGHT

LIGHT

inverted image
on film

because the image it captures

comes out upside down!

Another big problem?

The image will fade.

And that's where Daguerre's

big improvement was made.

Slipped into the camera
was a copper plate
bathed in iodine crystals.
(Its power was great!)

The plate copied an image
that no one could see
until mercury fumes
made it clear as could be.

To keep it from smudging,
Daguerre was then able
to soak it in water
plus salt from his table!

SAMUEL MORSE

1838

MESSAGES by WIRE

Before Morse, the mail traveled only by letter. But mail sent by wire moved much faster and better.

Pulses of current could work, in effect, to cause an electromagnet to deflect.

tap tap tap

The magnet moved an arm
that beat out a mode
of dashes and dots
we all call Morse code.

Our Congress approved
of Morse code and, what's more,
told Morse to string wires from
DC to Baltimore.

Telegraphs became
the latest sensation.
Soon telegraph wires
linked up the whole nation.

ALEXANDER GRAHAM BELL

1876
TELEPHONE

Son of a deaf mother,
Mr. Bell really cared
about improving the lives
of the hearing impaired.

mouthpiece

ear

His phonoautograph (PHOH-noh-AW-toh-graf)
used a real human ear
to *draw* sound vibrations
the deaf could read but not hear!

The gizmo led him to think maybe he could send off sounds by electricity.

His assistant, Tom Watson, receiver to ear, heard Bell, down the hall, transmit sound he could hear.

Watson, come here. I want to see you.

THOMAS EDISON
∂1877∂
PHONOGRAPH

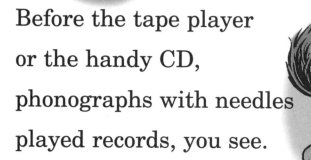

Before the tape player
or the handy CD,
phonographs with needles
played records, you see.

After improving Bell's telephone,
Edison had the intention
of making another
telephone invention.
It would copy down calls
so businesses could track
who had called up
and who to call back.

Just like your ear,
a receiver caught sound,
copied down by a needle
on a cylinder round.

foil around cylinder

"Mary had a little lamb....."

needle

flywheel

handle

In addition to messages,
it copied music and song,
and became all the rage
before very long.

GOTTLIEB DAIMLER
1886
FOUR-WHEELED AUTOMOBILE

A man named Daimler (DIME-ler), whom I will now mention, made a gas-fed internal combustion engine.

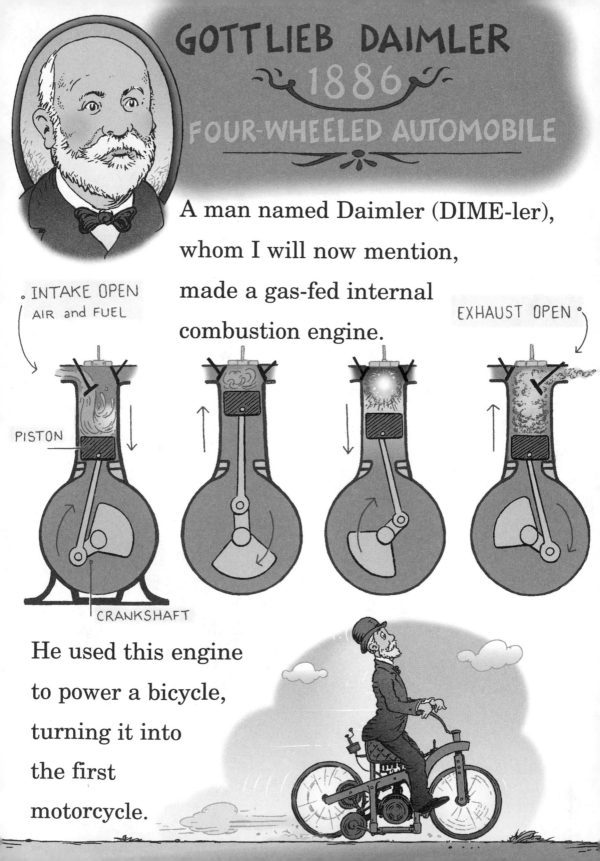

INTAKE OPEN
AIR and FUEL

EXHAUST OPEN

PISTON

CRANKSHAFT

He used this engine to power a bicycle, turning it into the first motorcycle.

Next he took a stagecoach
and unhitched the horse team,
then fit it with an engine.
NOW what was his scheme?

The wheels spun around,
and experts all feel
that this was the first
four-wheeled
automobile!

WILBUR and ORVILLE WRIGHT

1903

When motorized airplanes had all—so far—failed, the brothers Wright felt that they had the deal nailed.

Making wings shaped for flight was the Wrights' fondest goal, to allow for balance and flying control.

A movable rudder that fit on the rear was added to help the brothers to steer.

FIXED-WING MOTORIZED AIRCRAFT

On a hill in Kitty Hawk,
after many a try,
Wilbur one day
set out to fly. . . .

And 852 feet
in the air Wilbur flew!
He made like the birds
and made history, too!

MARY ANDERSON—1905

Once, streetcar drivers
in the rain and the snow
had to lean out the window
to see where to go.

Mary Anderson drew up,
and then she made,
an arm on a spring
with a smooth
rubber blade.

MANUALLY OPERATED WINDSHIELD WIPERS

The driver pulled a lever
to make the blade go
and sweep off the rain
and the slush and the snow.

GARRETT MORGAN
1923

Thing One just told me
a thing you should know:
our street traffic signals
once were just stop and go.

GO STOP

At busy intersections,
as you might well guess,
accidents would happen,
making quite a big mess!

But Garrett Morgan
thought it was a must
to give all these drivers
some time to adjust.
A signal could say:
In a moment or so,
you're expected to stop—
or expected to go.

1.

STOP / GO
STOP
STOP / GO

SPIN

2.

STOP
STOP
STOP
STOP

caution
for
oncoming
traffic
to slow
down

3.

GO / STOP
GO STOP / STOP

He invented a signal
that paused half the way
between go and stop,
like yellow lights of today.

35

COMPUTER INVENTORS "1936-2010"

In '36, Conrad Zuse (TSOO-zuh)
invented a machine:
the first working computer
the world's ever seen.

This computer had everything
a modern one has:
input, memory, process, output,
and all of that jazz!

"MACINTOSH—
1984"

"iPod—
2001"

Steve Jobs and his team
all get a big nod
for the Apple computer,
the iPad and iPod—
not to mention the iPhone,
which, as I understand,
is a computer
that fits in the hand!

"iPad—2010"

"iPhone—
2007"

TIM BERNERS-LEE

1989-90 - - - creates - -

A man who is really
no big-deal celeb
had a vision for something
called the World Wide Web.

This Web thing would have
no bosses or leaders.
Its contributors would be
its viewers, or readers.

His own computer,
which was brand NeXT,
set up a web of
computerized text.

WORLD WIDE WEB

Users added content
as they went along.
The Web was soon up
and it was going strong:
politics, facts, personal blogs,
home videos of kittens and dogs.

SPORTS

37-24

THE DAILY

SCIENCE
CHECK

SATURN

MY BLOG

TODAY

DICK

VID-TUBE

Tim Berners-Lee
(now read my lips)
put the knowledge
of the world
at your fingertips!

The Cat in the Hat

LEARNING LIBRARY

And speaking of tips,
I have one for you.
With a dream and a plan,
YOU can make gizmos, too.

And if stumped for ideas,
please don't forget that
you can put on my red-and-white
Cat's Thinking Hat!

GLOSSARY

Adjust: To prepare or get ready.

Content: Subjects or topics covered.

Contributors: Persons or things that give or add something.

Cylinder: A geometric shape with two circular flat ends.

Deflect: To change direction.

Electromagnet: A magnet powered by electrical current.

Fibers: The plant thread from which cloth is woven.

Fumes: Vapor, gas, or smoke.

Impaired: Flawed or damaged.

Input: The information fed into a computer.

Iodine crystals: A chemical from the ocean from which the moisture has dried.

Memory: Where information is stored in a computer.

Mercury: A toxic chemical element, also known as quicksilver.

Output: Information that comes out of a computer.

Piston: A cylinder that fits in a tube, where it moves to create power.

Process: When a computer follows steps that have been written for it.

Stock: A ready supply.

Transmit: To send information by electrical signal.

Vibrations: Quivering or shaking motions.

FOR FURTHER READING

Girls Think of Everything: Stories of Ingenious Inventions by Women by Catherine Thinmesh, illustrated by Melissa Sweet (HMH Books for Young Readers). An award-winning look at over fifty inventors, with illustrations done in vibrant collage. For ages 8–12.

So You Want to Be an Inventor? by Judith St. George, illustrated by David Small (Philomel). A fun, fact-filled picture book sure to inspire budding inventors! For ages 7 and up.

Thomas Edison: A Brilliant Inventor by the editors of *TIME for Kids* (HarperCollins, *TIME for Kids* Biographies). This NSTA-CBC Outstanding Science Trade Book is a great introduction to the famous inventor. For ages 6–10.

What Color Is My World? The Lost History of African-American Inventors by Kareem Abdul-Jabbar and Raymond Obstfeld, illustrated by Ben Boos and A. G. Ford (Candlewick). A story about a brother and sister exploring their new home and learning how many of the things in it were invented by African-Americans. For ages 8–12.

INDEX

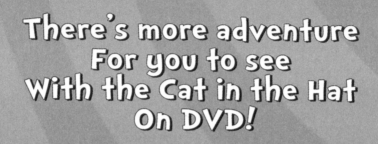